WHERE IS JUSTICE FOR BLESSED?

Blessed Kearns

Published by new Generation Publishing in 2023,
Copyright © BLESSED KEARNS 2023

First Edition

The author asserts the moral right under the Copyright, Designs and Patent Act 1988 to be identified as the author of this work.

All rights reserved. No part of this publication may be reproduced, stored in a retrieval system or transmitted, in any form or by any means without the prior consent of the author, nor be otherwise circulated in any form of binding or cover other than that which it is published and without a similar condition being imposed on the subsequent purchaser.

ISBN

    Paperback 978-1-80369-894-6
    Hardback: 978-1-80369-895-3
    Ebook: 978-1-80369-896-0

www.newgeneration-publishing.com

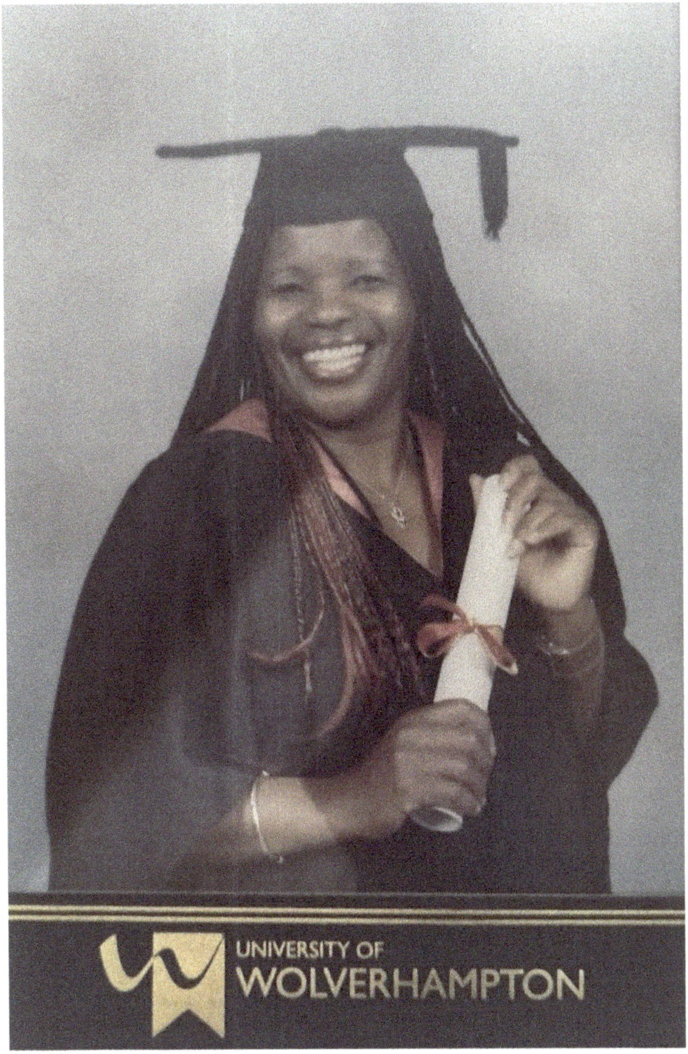
UNIVERSITY OF
WOLVERHAMPTON

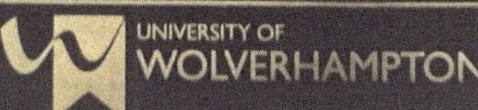

List of Contents

1. Foreword 1
2. Suspension 5
3. The Transcript 7
4. Allegations 13
5. Investigations 17
6. Terms of Contract 27
7. Tribunal 30
8. Admitted to Hospital 33
9. Afterword: On Reflection of My Past 35

Foreword

In March 2007 I saw an advert in the paper for staff nurses in Oxford, and so I decided to apply for the job. A short time after, I was called for an interview with a ward manager and the charge nurse.

Within a month I got word to say that I had been successful and had got the job, but I was still living in the West Midlands and working as a Registered Mental Health Nurse. I had to inform my manager that I had got a job in Oxford, and it was still under NHS, as I still needed to fulfil my contract deal with NHS for two years.

I then started looking for another house in Oxford, which was difficult as I had to find a home within my budget and in the right location. In 2008 I bought a two-bedroom maisonette, with a kitchen. The property needed decorating, and initially it was still under lease, so it would take time before the deal went through.

I had been living with my sister who was working in Oxford. I did not own a car, so decided to take some driving lessons in order to be able to drive to work. I was tired of getting the bus, which was often late, and would cause problems if I failed to get to work on time in order to make the handover from the nightshift member of staff.

I learned about *click bait*, whereby you had to know someone to get promoted or to climb the ladder. I used to get along fine with my colleagues, then rumour had it that I was paying them money, which was not true and a very painful pill for me to swallow. I was being constantly undermined as a student mentor, even though I had been educated at Oxford University.

Although the working environment could be difficult at times, I enjoyed working there, and I felt that my training to be a nurse had been worthwhile.

Some people can be difficult to work with; they have their own issues, but some of them were good people. I saw good nurses leaving, which was due to the lack of support they were receiving or the fact they simply needed to earn more money elsewhere to be able to afford their standard of living.

When we worked as a team, then all was well. There were some good people amongst my work colleagues, who were just there to do their job and pay their bills. I tried to do my best while working with the service users, and I gave them the respect that they were due, but click bait was crippling the department.

On reflection, I cannot remember an occasion when my manager called me into the office and thanked me for my hard work. A little thank you would have gone a long way. I know I was getting paid to do my job, but I believed that my manager was responsible for ensuring that a strong team mentality existed between us all, which was certainly not the case. There was so much prejudice.

There were times when I had to put on a brave face in order to do my job. I needed to be strong and less judgemental, and more over I did not discriminate, although I felt discriminated. I realized that if you did not dance to their music, then you were out. This woman claimed she was in love with me, and everyone knew it, which was extremely difficult.

I suffered bullying, which was not dealt with by the management team. I voiced my concerns, but they failed to do anything about it, and so the torment continued. This began to affect my work. I would dread having to work with her each day, which could make it a long, drawn-out day, even if she was in the office for most of the time. I was made to work more than the others, and still, nothing was done about it. I even asked if I could be transferred to another ward, but my request was declined.

The environment and the culture were toxic, but nothing was done about it. I was viewed as a moron in front of my peers.

Backward and Feeble-Minded Children, 1912. – "Those whose mental development is above that of an imbecile but does not exceed that of a normal child of about twelve years." – Edmund Burke Huey

I continued to put on a brave face at work, but the torment carried on. It was hurting me mentally, and some of the staff would be quite supportive, and tell me not to worry, and that they all knew what she was like. But I found it difficult to deal with, and more so knowing that she would be pleasant to other members of staff, which surprised me. When she wanted a shift to be covered, she would ask me; if another member of staff phoned in sick, she would ask me to cover that shift. And even if I covered the shift, it did not stop her from undermining me. I requested a meeting to see if we could work better together, perhaps resolve any issues by way of mediation. She was reluctant to do this, however, it was agreed that a meeting would take place to resolve any issues, but nothing came of it. In fact, it only made matters worse.

Things were starting to get on top of me, so I made the request for a career break. My request was denied.

Psychological projection can be utilized as a means of obtaining or justifying certain actions that would normally be found atrocious or heinous. This often means projecting false accusations, information, etc., onto an individual for the sole purpose of maintaining a self-created illusion, e.g., that I was paying to have a quiet shift, which was absurd. Policies and protocol were not being followed:

Do not bully other members of staff regardless of your position and do not abuse your position.

I was being treated unfairly on a regular basis and the gossip was malicious and the rumours about me were unfounded. I was constantly being undermined and this hurt me. We all go through difficulties at times, and we all deal with matters differently. Therefore, we should never judge people, just support them and respect their positions.

Nursing is not cut out for everyone; you need to be patient and to able to work as a team with the right people. You need to be strong and less judgemental, and more over not to discriminate.,

It had become intolerable for me to function properly at work. I had tried requesting a transfer to Bullingdon for six months, which would mean having to travel further, but I had a car. This was how bad things had got, and I witnessed newly trained staff being offered more opportunities and even promotion just like that.

Suspension

I was shocked at the allegations and could not understand what was going on. I walked down the corridor, my heart beating fast and my mind racing in different directions. I just could not understand what was going on. When I finally arrived at her office, I was told to take a seat and then hand over the keys to the medication cupboard, even though I was the only qualified nurse on duty that day. I had just been getting ready to do the handover for the late shift when I was told to pick up any belongings before being escorted off the ward.

My mind had gone blank, and my body had gone numb. I could not think straight as I got into my car, and then started to cry thinking that my whole world had fallen apart.

When I got home, I called my ex-boyfriend and told him what had just happened. He advised me to call my manager back, and I did so, and she just informed me that I would be receiving a letter soon. I thanked her and then ended the call, but I could not accept what was happening.

I received a letter the 2nd May, which clearly outlined that I had been suspended with immediate effect. The term 'immediate effect' confused me as I had been at work on the 29th April and off duty the next day, which left me confused as to what discussions had taken place and how they had had arrived at that decision.

I had been suspended indefinitely so it seemed, and during this time there had been a number of investigations.

Lord Justice Elias: *"Suspension should be a last resort after all other reasonable options have been considered. For example, a temporary adjustment to the employee's working arrangements can remove the need to suspend, e.g. being moved to a different area of the workplace."*

The reason for an employee being on suspension should be reviewed on an ongoing basis and be timebound. In the judgment, Lord Justice Elias made some additional comments which are of great interest to employers. "In a shorter time frame and that consideration should have been given to the unblemished service of some 20 years by each of the two nurses. "During the time I was seeing my GP who referred me to a psychologist; we had several meetings once a week and my sickness record went through the roof. I was struggling. I knew that I needed to attend these sessions on time but I had to drag myself out of bed each morning. I felt like a fly in a jar which had a lid on, and I felt nobody was listening to me. I felt destroyed and the anger inside became toxic. My doctor was worried about me, and he had advised me to seek counselling as he was concerned that I might kill myself or do something stupid, but I reassured him this was not going to be the case. I knew my children would never forgive me if I did that, but I was struggling, so he prescribed antidepressants and a sleeping pill called zopiclone. I was struggling to cope and I just needed to be alone.

The Transcript

Q. As you will see, the statement is not signed or dated. I wonder if you could be happy to sign and date it now if you believe that the contents and statement are true?

A. *Yes*

Q. It is the 2nd June today then there are other statements that I have you is entitled referring to her name

A. *Yes*

Q. That is a seven-page document?

A. *Yes*

Q. I would be grateful if you could verify that the contents are true to the best of your knowledge, and then sign and date?

A. *On every page?*

Q. Would the panel be satisfied-----

CHAIRMEN: the final page will be fine.
All the documents which were signed and dated were taken and accepted as evidence by the NMC.
A lot of questions were asked to her by the panel with regards to the investigation, and some of the evidence remained in a draft form. It was mentioned also, that it was believed she had taken on a full-time contract with the home.

Q. I just want to be clear about this policy document: where is it kept and how it is it transmitted to people working for the Trust?

A. *The policy documents are all kept on the Trust internet in the policy section under the Human Resources Policy.*

Q. And when would someone, who is working for the Trust, be introduced to this policy?

A. *There is a sort of online list of policies that some of you must be aware of. I am not fully versed on the carer's break policy, and whether it is one that you have to say that you have read or whether it is just one that is listed and need to be aware of.* When this was discussed, it transpired I was a not given this policy as it was not available during that time, and I was not given a copy as the manager informed the panel.

The discussions were made addressing the carer's break policy, and no live policy was upheld within the disciplinary process because there was no actual working policy at that time.

Barrister: Questions and Answers

I just want to ask some questions by your classifications. Now very helpfully you just answered a question regarding the sessional contracts, with my learned friend but can I ask you this.

Q. Where would she sign on a contractual basis, to say that she had that sessional contract as well as the full-time contract; would there be a contract for that?

- For the sessional shifts there is a separate kind of appointment form that is signed the sessional contract was help prior to the career break, because can hold full-time contract with the Trust and then a sessional contract to do some extra shifts on top of the career break so she would have been working on that sessional contract that already existed.

Q. *So, would that be a contract for her full-time post and a separate contract for her sessional post?*

A. Yes.

Q. *Okay, we have talked about documents, so just for clarification, there is an Employment Break Policy?*

A. Yes, I think that is what it is called, yes.

Q. *And we have seen that at page 108, well, I think it actually starts a bit earlier than that in the contract? Where do you find that?*

A. I think, in terms of when… That wording is possibly not…when I was giving the statement, I was referring to a specific policy the Trust, move it was clear---

Q. *Well, you said in your statement "the trust policy on secondary employment is quite clear…" so what policy are you referring to?*

A. I have not…because there was not a Working Times Policy live, which again in the disciplinary investigation, because this was at the early stages and my understanding that the Trust policy, but then when we completed the investigation , as the investigation report outlines, there is not, other than the Career Break Policy where it states an (sic)would not normally be able to take employment somewhere else. There was another policy where I could that it stated. So that was in the initial statement when I had spoken to the NMC but I was at early stages of the investigation.

Q. *So the only place where you would find the policy on secondary employment is in the Working Time Policy (the Weaver Policy), is that correct or I am mistaken about that?*

A. I do not … off the top of my head I do not know. I can remember in terms of whether, in the Waiver Policy, it has in it there.

Q. *Well, let us just have a look at that then, it is at page 88. That starts page 1 0f 8 at the bottom "Working Time Policy" and that is where the director and the staff side lead have been signed something. I presume that is for everybody.*

A. Yeah, the issue with this policy was that this policy was not live at the point that this all took place which was why it was not acknowledged that this policy would not have been available and was not live at that point.

Q. Right, so Ms Kearns could not have checked about the Working Times Policy then at that point?

A. No.

Q. Where is says I am in particular page, 93 that is in the section "The 48 Hours Working Week"?

A. Yeah that is correct. So, during the process of the investigation, that is where it became clear that this policy was not live, therefore, it was acknowledged, within the investigation report and therefore, at the disciplinary that this, although it states it in this policy it was not live at the time therefore it was not fact.

THIS IS A TRANSCIPT FROM THE MNC WHEN I ATTENDED

Q. Now you say she also had a contract for full-time employment and part-time employment, is there any mention in any of the contracts about secondary employment, working times, that she would be directed to or would have available to her that you are aware of?

A. No, I did. As part of the investigation, I did look at the contracts to see whether there would be anything, but we did not find anything, which is why it was obviously not the...

Q. Right. Perhaps we can just have a look at that contract on page 76... so this is the "Terms and Conditions of employment". Now is not signed or date and this a copy.

Regarding issues relating work:

Q. There is a member of that Ms Kearns was having some issues with and her name was not mentioned directly and was asked if he was aware of this?

A. I was aware of there was having some issues sort of equally from both sides but not that that in anywhere linked to the career break or that there had been sort of current issues that time but there had previously been difficulties which had addressed in relation to both of them and equally sort on both sides it was difficult,

Q. *It is correct, is it not there was some questions over whether you were the appropriate person to investigate this case, given that you were this this member of staff line manager?*

A. Yeah that is correct.

Q *You agree with that as we can that page 24 that is the report .You see there at the top, " it felt like the BK and SA that is (sic) was appropriate that MD investigate this case on grounds that MD was the line manager.... And would not be impartial. "However, it appears like you did continue to investigate.*

A. Yes that decision was not made by me. That decision was made elsewhere.

Q *No, yes, I can see that. And just for clarification at page 68 which is the interview with Ms Kearns we can see that she actually mentioned, in June---and I am looking at particularly at page 70 now the very top of page 70 where Ms Kearns said "I love my job in T/H. There have been pockets of lots of issues between me and ... name not given . You that is MD" that is ... was aware of some things. It was not done in a nice way. I felt this is why I asked for career break. I came and asked for a career break at the end of November / December time ". Then you said later down the page half down. I understand there were difficulties, but name not given So there was some admission then that the reason was that she was feeling in her words picked on and you were aware that there were difficulties between them.?*

A. Yes

Q. *We know and Ms Kearns admits it, some issues ...sorry that she did ask for as for a career break because her partner in being up in Manchester having been unwell and had been aware of that had you?*

A. I had been aware sort of several years earlier that her partner had been unwell and obviously, at the time of career break it became--- I was then aware that again he was unwell again but I was not aware that continued to be unwell for that time.

Q okay .*Now it is correct, is it not following all the investigations and disciplinary Ms Kearns is now working back at the Trust? T/H.*

A. Yes at T/H but my understanding is Blessed has not been back into work since the disciplinary but some reasons.

Q. so, she told you the nature of the health condition?

A. We did not go into lots of detail but just that he was unwell having sort of further tests and needed—she needed to be with him to support him at that time.

Q. *Thank you. I relation to working back-to-back shift, is that acceptable?*

A. No guess would never roster somebody to work that. We would never expect somebody to work that we would never allow somebody to work that. But there is not anywhere stated that not working time policy neither at the time and there neither stated whereby that's not allowed so it was only on the reasonable ness which is why was only partially up held.

Q you are answering a wrong question to the one I asked a

A. sorry

Q. *I think you have you have your management hat on, and I am asking is working back-to-back shifts acceptable? I am asking the "Working times Policy", I am asking you.*

Allegations

This is a letter dated November 2014 which had more allegations.

1. To establish whether BK has been working full time for another employer in addition to her full-time contract with the Trust.

2. To establish whether any such employment represents a breach of the Working Time Regulations or the Trust Code of Conduct (policy reference Corp 13) or the Trust Contract of Employment.

3. To clarify the circumstances of the complaint against BK recently raised with NMC, and in particular, to establish whether these complaints indicate clinical practice that may present a risk to patients care.

4. To investigate the veracity and authenticity of any reference apparently originating from the Trust enabling BK to obtain employment with another employer.

5. To establish whether any of these allegations are compatible to BK's employment as a Staff Nurse working with vulnerable adults.

6. To establish whether any of these allegations may represent a breach of MNC Code.

I was suspended on **hearsay as** evidence of this horrible suspension, the MD informed the Trust I was working for them on a full-time contract; referring to two days hearsay evidence means whatever a person is heard to say, includes: a statement made by a person, not called as witness; a statement contained or recorded in any book, document or record which is not admissible. The general rule is that hearsay evidence is not admissible in a court of law.

> Appendix 13
>
> Met with Blessed
> 2/5/14 - Suspended due to concerns about working 2 full-time jobs.
>
> Blessed states - Didn't have a permanent contract with care home.
> - only worked 3 days at care home
> - They did offer her post but she wasn't sure if she should take it.
>
> 2/5/14 - spoke to Michelle Daly (manager at care home)
> Blessed working on a permanent contract.
> Full time 42hr per week
> Started 28/11/13 - left 8/1/14
> - employed as lead nurse in charge of Dementia Care
> - Stated that she was a lead nurse with managerial responsibilities in her current role when applied for post at the care home.

Section 60 of the Evidence Act states that oral evidence must be direct. R v Horncastle was an English legal case concerning the rules on Hearsay Evidence. The appellants claimed that English law on hearsay evidence violated Article 6 of the European Convention on Human Rights (ECHR) according to decisions of the European Court of Human Rights (ECtHR). The UK's Supreme Court dismissed the appeal.

The House of Lords had said that UK courts should follow 'clear and constant' decisions of the ECtHR, yet the Lords also agreed that the HRA did not change the rules of precedent in the UK. Therefore, how far UK courts should follow the ECtHR was a 'hot topic'.

How can one hold full-time contract for two employers, was above me? I did not have a contract with either of them. A contract is offered for permanent positions, and usually set out the employee's salary or hourly wage. Other details included within a full-time contract include holiday entitlements, pension benefits, parental leave allowances, and details on Statutory Sick Pay. This is the document that binds you for taking any employment somewhere else, then I was suspended for a document which was not even given to me in the beginning, and not only that I had been working there for an exceptionally long time.

During these meetings I was supported by a lady from Unison, who I will always be grateful for. There was no evidence to support their allegations that I was working full time for the Trust and there was no contract of employment between me and the S/H. I had worked for two days and then I was on annual leave during that time.

This was not full-time work, it was merely work on a casual basis.

I was aware that other staff members within the Trust who had contracts of employment with other employers had not been put through a disciplinary process like me.

With this I was put though a disciplinary process unfairly. He commented that it appears to be the almost automatic response of employers to allegations of this kind to suspend the employees concerned, and to forbid them from contacting anyone, as soon as a complaint is made; irrespective of the likelihood of the complaint being established. He said that a suspension should *"not be a knee jerk reaction, and it will be a breach of the duty of trust and confidence towards the employee if it is"*. An employee will frequently feel belittled and demoralised by the total exclusion from work and the enforced removal from their work colleagues, many of whom will be friends. This can be psychologically very damaging and raise the prospect of guilt before a full investigation has been undertaken. Therefore, a decision to suspend an employee should not be taken lightly and should be for no longer than is reasonably necessary giving consideration to all the facts surrounding the matter. I was stressed, and I could not sleep.

Investigations

Dated November 2014

In clear view of the date of suspension and time of investigation, I would like to lodge a grievance, as this is now influencing my mental health.

During the investigation there was no contact and I ended up discussing this issue with the Unison lady who was supporting me.

According to the hospital protocols. A suspension decision should not be more than two weeks by the manager who instigated the suspension, and the review to be confirmed in writing by the employee. The manager who is investigating these allegations should be impartial.

One of the countless allegations was based on hearsay as evidence.

Hearsay is inadmissible, meaning that it is not permitted to go before a jury or magistrates at a trial as evidence to prove a matter, either for the prosecution or the defence. I was suspended for hearsay as evidence of this horrible suspension:

When I attended the Nursing and Midwifery Council (NMC) there were so many allegations, some of which had originated from this home I went to do extra shifts for two days, when I was on my annual leave. I wanted a bit of extra cash as I had just bought a house, but it wasn't a full-time contract, so I failed to understand the problem.

I loved my job so much. I enjoyed doing what I was doing, and I did this passionately. But I was struggling mentally; I had no support, and I had to try to find six thousand pounds to pay my barrister. I never received any support from the Trust, which shocked the panel at the NMC. I was suffering mentally, and I was crying constantly as I had to live with this stain on my life when

I was not guilty of any wrongdoing. It was so painful having to deal with these false accusations as all I wanted to do was to get back to work, however, the cliques were causing me a lot of problems, and I was out as far as they were concerned.

Once I got there, I realised I was not the only nurse who had reservations over the job anymore due to a lack of support from the NMC. It was a sad situation, but I had concerns of my own.

I had taken the suspension personally and it was such a difficult time for me, I couldn't sleep. I couldn't pull myself away from my depression, and I thought of the words that my lecturer had spoken to me: *"Look after your PIN number as there will be vultures out there to take it away from you."* I was in this dark hole and I was hurting, and the tears never stopped running down my face.

During that time there were two managers: one from the home where I did extra hours and the other was from the Trust where I was supposed to be fully employed. She also had allegations of her own, which I had been suspended for. There had been six allegations made since I had been suspended, while the allegation of me having two full-time contracts had been imposed upon me. I was suffering with depression, and I did not want people to see me this way.

At times when power is used against you, you feel helpless, and always on your own. It was a terrible time. I was not well mentally, and boy, was I struggling during that agonizing meeting. I had studied to be a nurse for three years, and this had come as a bitter pill to swallow. I was devastated.

I was prescribed antidepressant Citalopram and Zopiclone to help me to sleep but this did not work. I was sinking very deep, I could not even leave the house, and I was constantly on the computer. I could not sleep, and I felt like I was drowning, and I did not want anybody near me. I spoke to my daughter who lived in London, and she came to see me. I had lost the Internet and now I couldn't afford to keep my car, and I had to watch as it was towed away.

I went through counselling sessions. That also took time, repeatedly trying to find my way out of this. I was angry, mainly with myself, and I realised that I was psychologically damaged. this was a difficult journey. I read a lot of other cases that were related to what I was going through, as well finding out how others coped during suspension.

I was hurting, and I told myself it was suspension that went wrong, and this nearly destroyed me. I was extremely unwell.

It felt like I was being hunted down, as if I had killed someone. It was now 2015 and I had watched my nursing career plummet after spending three years at university and with nothing to show for it.

My brain was shutting down on me, I was so tired. I visualized my mother, and then thought about the person who was bulling me at work, and right in front of the manager at that time, although bullying was admitted under oath.

My ex-boyfriend encouraged my barrister to bring this up, which she was reluctant in doing so at first, but she did, and it was admitted. I couldn't believe it; all this time the manager knew about what I was going through but never even tried to intervene. The time had come for me to resign from the job I loved. I did not make this decision lightly, but I knew it had to be done.

To work in such an industry demands teamwork, and I had now reached the point during my suspension when the bullying against me had now been substantiated. I was emotional, but the stain on my career remained.

Even if one is rich, successful, famous, or "has it all", the psychological devastation can be ruinous. If you are not believed, if you cannot fight back with the true story, if now you are distrusted and under scrutiny, the sense of helplessness is overwhelming. People with inner vulnerabilities are easy targets. Others sense the fragility and find it thrilling to gang up or attack. Having a scapegoat can help a group form a strong bond and find meaning in what could be otherwise empty lives.

It is widely known that people with certain kinds of pathology are brilliant at looking like victims when they are perpetrators. They can ruin the life of an innocent person. And this is what happened to me; with so many false accusations, my emotions took over, and I could not pull myself up. I could not come to terms with the reasons behind all this, whereas I am usually a very strong person.

On my understanding of the MNC, they deal with pills, and not employment disputes, which is where the confusion remains. I was accused of sleeping with one of my colleagues, who was brave enough to give evidence to dispute that claim.

I had made complaints about the person who had been bullying me, but this was never dealt with appropriately.

All these allegations and groundless rules were false but were thrown at me. According to the law when one person makes false accusations against or statements about another and "publishes" those statements (by transmitting them to a third party by written word or word of mouth), and those statements damage the reputation, character or integrity of that person, in relation to full time contract of which both could not produce or give, these documents were sent to NMC.

With an intent to damage my reputation as a Registered Mental Health Nurse, I started my search for other work. I tried to focus on my mental health and wellbeing as stated in Maslow's hierarchy, characterising human portrait as the shape of a pyramid, with the largest, most fundamental needs at the bottom, and transcendence at the top.

In other words, the idea is that the individual's most basic needs must be met before they become motivated to achieve higher-level needs, which I needed.

The most fundamental four layers of the pyramid contain what Maslow called "deficiency needs" or "d-needs": esteem, friendship and love, security, and physical needs. If these "deficiency needs" are not met – except for the most fundamental (physiological) need – there may not be a physical indication, but the individual will feel anxious and tense. Deprivation is what causes deficiency, so when one has unmet needs, this motivates them to fulfil what they are being denied. Maslow's idea suggests that the most basic level of needs must be met before the individual will strongly desire (or focus motivation upon) the secondary or higher-level needs. Maslow also coined the term "meta motivation".

During my torturous suspension, they did not follow their own policies, or should I say they did not abide by them. It felt like there was something they wanted from me, but there was nothing more I could do.

These false allegations destroyed me and there was nobody who I could turn to. It felt like I was being punished for something I didn't do. The medication and supervision stopped, without any explanation. I used to drive services uses out on leave in a unit car, yet I had been informed that I was not supposed to be dealing with medication, which baffled me. The clique culture had singled me out and I was not wanted there.

In light of the court hearings, Human Resources had disregarded my latest pay review, which was just another case of discrimination towards me. The law protects you against discrimination at work, including dismissal, employment terms and conditions, pay and benefits, promotion and transfer opportunities, training and recruitment.

I read a lot of issues relating to me. I was hurting, and I told myself it was a suspension that had gone wrong, and this nearly destroyed me. Even to this day I am still puzzled as to what went on and I have not found the answers I need.

This made me seek for other employment and I was willing to relocate from Oxford and go somewhere else. But this wouldn't be easy as I had just bought a house. I was about to jump from the frying pan and straight into the fire.

"It is important not to suppress your feelings altogether when you are depressed. It is equally important to avoid terrible arguments or expressions of outrage. You should steer clear of emotionally damaging behaviours. People forgive, but it is best not to stir things up to the point at which forgiveness is required. When you are depressed, you need the love of other people, and yet depression fosters actions that destroy that love. Depressed people often stick pins into their own life rafts. The conscious mind can intervene. One is not helpless." – Andrew Solomon

The Berlin Wall was a guarded concrete barrier that physically and ideologically divided Berlin from 1961 to 1989. Construction of the wall was commenced by the German Democratic Republic on 13 August 1961. The Wall cut off West Berlin from surrounding East Germany, including East Berlin. The barrier included guards, accompanied by a wide area that contained anti-vehicle trenches, beds of nails and other defences.

The Eastern Bloc portrayed the Wall as protecting its population from fascist elements conspiring to prevent the "will of the people" from building a socialist state in East Germany.

I was crumbling mentally. I had lost everything and now I needed time to heal and to get back on my feet again. Suddenly, I had become a nobody.

Sigmund Freud said, *"The pain of the ego is the worst kind of pain. Kids who are scapegoated with words that cause unbearable humiliation sometimes commit suicide."* Due to working in that difficult environment we needed to offer support, not to humiliate each other.

I was wounded. I could do any nursing anymore. *"The human spirit is more powerful than any drug—and that is what needs to be nourished: with work, play, friendship, family. These are the things that matter."* – Robin Williams. I needed to heal.

"A supervisor in analytic school told me that kids who are tortured with words are often more traumatized than those who have been physically abused." – Sigmund Freud

May (1976) considered Power against to be oppressive and damaging to service users which thus takes a form of a punishment. Smith (2008) pointed out that this theory is like French and Raven's coercive power which is always in a position to punish.

According to research, it is believed The Healing Process is a new independent service formed to enable individuals who feel they have suffered bullying or harassment in the past while working for the NHS. Highland Emotions—especially the dark and dishonoured ones—hold a tremendous amount of energy. We have all seen what happens when we repress or blindly express them. With *the Language of Emotions,* empathic counsellor Karla McLaren shows you how to meet your emotion and receive their life-saving wisdom to safely move toward resolution and equilibrium. Through experiential exercises covering a full spectrum of feelings from anger, fear, and shame to jealousy, grief, joy, and more, you will discover how to work with your own and others' emotions with fluency and expertise. Although this was extremely difficult.

On my return from the NMC, I had requested for my money to be paid, but this did not happen, even after contacting ACAS and requesting their assistance. I was told by Human Resources that I was going to get my money, as the case had not been settled.

I had also gone through the Care Quality Commission, who did nothing to help me. Any evidence that would have supported my case had just vanished into thin air. Nursing is not cut out for everyone, and I found this to be true. Emotions, empathic counsellor Karla McLaren shows you *"how to meet your emotions and receive their life-saving wisdom to safely move toward resolution and equilibrium. Through experiential exercises covering a full spectrum of feelings from anger, fear, and shame to jealousy, grief, joy, and more, you will discover how to work with your own and others"*.

When I left my job, I had not been paid my final month's salary, which I took up with ACAS. I found this to be an atrocious act on their behalf, especially after the false accusations that had been aimed at me.

Narcissistic personality disorder (NPD) involves a pattern of self-centred, arrogant thinking and behaviour, a lack of empathy and consideration for other people, and an excessive need for admiration. Others often describe people with NPD as cocky, manipulative, selfish, patronizing, and demanding. This way of thinking and behaving surfaces in every area of the narcissist's life: from work and friendships to family and love relationships.

It's important to remember that narcissists aren't looking for partners; they're looking for obedient admirers. At times one could do extra work to cover when there were not enough staffing levels. I was getting paid; my efforts were not recognised.

Healthy relationships are based on mutual respect and caring. But narcissists aren't capable of true reciprocity in their relationships. It isn't just that they're not willing; they truly aren't able. They don't see you. Even NMC noticed this during their cross-examination protocols which were not followed.

False accusations are similar to being bullied. Even if one is rich, successful, famous, or "has it all", the psychological devastation can be ruinous. If you are not believed, if you cannot fight back with the true story, if now you are distrusted and under scrutiny, the sense of helplessness is overwhelming. People with inner vulnerabilities are easy targets. Others sense the fragility and find it thrilling to gang up or attack. Having a scapegoat can help a group form a strong bond and find meaning in what could be otherwise empty lives.

It is widely known that people with certain kinds of pathology are brilliant at looking like victims when they are perpetrators. They can ruin the life of an innocent person. And this is what happened to me. with so much false accusations I left my emotions take over, I could not pull myself up.

I was informed that by whistleblowing, then the court would afford me merits. However, giving the timing of it all, I was told that any additional claims from me now would be deemed late and therefore they would be struck off. I gave names but nothing came of it, which I found astonishing.

I had no money and I tried to contact NHS England on several occasions. My health was not so good, and I was falling deeper into depression.

The painful part about being found to be guilty was that I was not fit to do my job. *"You are guilty and not fit to be a nurse, Miss Kearns,"* were the words that echoed in my mind.

I read a lot of issues relating to me and the case; I was hurting, and I told myself it was the suspension that had gone wrong, and this nearly destroyed me. I got extremely sick, both mentally and physically. I had to live with the false allegations every day; I was living with this dark cloud that did not want to shift. It took a long time to try to put everything behind me.

It had been very difficult working at the hospital, and there were times when I broke down and cried uncontrollably. The NMC investigate complaints regarding the following:
- Misconduct.
- Lack of competence.
- Not having the necessary knowledge of English.
- Criminal behaviour.
- Serious ill health.

I remember thinking I was someone's child and I wondered what my own mother would think of me and whether she would say that I was an orphan. I was crying and hurting. I was my mother's child, who was trying to work hard. I knew my capabilities, but the constant bullying had been getting to me. I had been undermined and given more duties to perform than the others. Even when the ward had been short staffed, I had been called upon to do above and beyond my normal workload.

Terms of the Contract

> Dear Blessed,
> Please see attached a copy of the Trust's only Working Time Policy. I have checked your file and unfortunately we do not hold a copy of a sign-out/waiver form. I have attached a copy of our standard contract of emplo[yment]
> I have requested that a contract is issued to you for signature and return.
> I have asked ▇ to check your file on the ward for an opt out form and v

Employees and employers must stick to a contract until it ends (for example, by an employer or employee giving notice or an employee being dismissed) or until the terms are changed (usually by agreement between the employee and employer).

If a person has an agreement to do some work for someone (like paint their house), this isn't an employment contract but a 'contract to provide services'.

Libel: Libel is a defamation that is written, such as in a newspaper, magazine or on the internet.

The defamation damaged his character in some way (document reveals that I had signed a full-time contract with another employer, which was absurd).

Psychological projection can be utilized as a means of obtaining or justifying certain actions that would normally be found atrocious or heinous. This often means projecting false accusations, information, etc., onto an individual for the sole purpose of maintaining a self-created illusion; narcissistic personality disorder involves a pattern of self-centred, arrogant thinking and behaviour, a lack of empathy and consideration for other people, and an excessive need for admiration.

Others often describe people with NPD as cocky, manipulative, selfish, patronizing, and demanding. This way of thinking and behaving surfaces in every area of the narcissist's life: from work and friendships to family and love relationships. It's important to remember that narcissists aren't looking for partners; they're looking for obedient admirers.

Re: CQC – The Care Act 2014: safeguarding adults sets out a clear legal framework for how local authorities and other parts of the system should protect adults at risk of abuse or neglect. Local authorities have new safeguarding duties. They must lead a multi-agency local adult safeguarding system that looks to prevent abuse and neglect and stop it quickly when it happens. Safeguarding someone with care and support in need dies because of neglect or abuse, and there is a concern that the local authority or its partners could have done more to protect them.

This Safeguarding Vulnerable Groups was passed to help avoid harm, or risk of harm, by preventing people who are deemed unsuitable to work with children and vulnerable adults from gaining access to them through their work.

The Being Open is a principle and ethical duty of openness, which applies to all incidents and any failure in care or treatment.

The Duty of Candour applies to incidents whereby moderate harm, significant harm or death has occurred.

It is a matter of judgment that needs to be exercised on a case-by-case basis to determine whether an incident that meets the Duty of Candour criteria has occurred. What may not appear to be such an incident at the outset may look vastly different once more information comes to light.

The Care Act 2014 places a general duty on local authorities to promote the wellbeing of individuals when conducting care and support functions. The definition of wellbeing includes:

- personal dignity including treating individuals with respect;
- physical and mental health and emotional wellbeing;
- protection from abuse and neglect.

(Department of Health, 2014)

Safeguarding Vulnerable Groups Act 2006 and the Protection of Freedoms Bill

This Safeguarding Vulnerable Groups Act 2006 was passed, to help avoid harm, or risk of harm, by preventing people who are deemed unsuitable to work with children and vulnerable adults from gaining access to them through their work.

An important part of promoting dignity is ensuring a working environment that encourages people to challenge practices in their own workplace. The law offers some protection from victimization to people who blow the whistle under the Public Interest Disclosure Act 1998.

If a criminal offence has been committed, or is being committed, the Public Concern at Work is a charity which has been the UK's leading authority on whistleblowing for the last 25 years. Their aim is to promote the concept of "stop harm sooner, by speaking up safely". Which I did.

Tribunal

Lawyers conducting litigation owe a divided loyalty. They have a duty to their clients, but they may not win by whatever means. They also owe a duty to the court and the administration of justice. They may not mislead the court or allow the judge to take sides. Every lawyer should be familiar with the words of Lord Hoffmann: "Nobody is above the law mainly when focusing on protecting the vulnerable adult in view of the case. Justice in its broadest sense is the principle that people receive which the 'deserving' being an impact upon numerous fields, more in a mental health setting."

The primary legal responsibility for safeguarding vulnerable adults lies with local authorities. A group of people need to come together to find the best ways to protect vulnerable adults, working within the principles of partnership and accountability.

There can be no secrets and no hiding place when it comes to exposing the abuse of vulnerable adults. The Government's White Paper, 'Modernising Social Services', published at the end of 1998, signalled our intention to provide better protection for individuals needing care and support. This is being taken up through the Care Standards Bill. We are also committed to providing greater protection to victims and witnesses, and the Government is actively implementing the measures proposed in 'Speaking Up for Justice', the report on the treatment of vulnerable or intimidated witnesses in the criminal justice system. Then if so, why were my complaints not noted, as I followed all the guidelines and policies? Why?

Again, with so many viewpoints and perspectives including the concepts of moral correctness based on ethics, rationale, law, religion equity and fairness the state will sometimes endeavour to increase justice with operating courts and enforce rulings. As the court is a person or institution based on fair judgement and transparent in all angles.

Although a legal representative is bound to strive to win a case, the lawyer must do so without in any way seeking to evade the rules intended to safeguard the administration of justice.

That report recognised that there were concerns about both the identification and reporting of crime against vulnerable adults in care settings, and endorsed the proposals made by the Association of Directors of Social Services, and others, that a national policy should be developed for the protection of vulnerable adults. It was agreed that local multi-agency codes of practice would be the best way forward. The development of these codes of practice should be co-ordinated locally by each local authority social services department. Hence trying to do what I believed was the best interest for the service users under the Mental Act.

To support this process this guidance is being issued under Section 7 of the Local Authority Social Services Act 1970. Government departments have worked closely together on the preparation of this guidance, and we commend it to local authority social services departments, the police service, and the health service.

An ex-junior lawyer, who was struck off after lying, is appealing against the Solicitors Disciplinary Tribunal's decision. was a newly qualified solicitor for this company when she lost a briefcase with sensitive documents when she accidentally left it on a train. She did not immediately report the loss to her supervisor at work, saying instead that she had left the documents at home. She confessed just over a week after the incident.

"Whether you provide health or social care, develop or manage social housing, deliver emergency services, or regulate complex professions, we're able to help you to deliver services to your communities."

So, what about the vulnerable adults? I have tried to be their voice. Who will be there for them?

"Women, like me, should try to do the impossible. And when they fail, their failure should be a challenge to others." – Amelia Earheart.

Admitted to Hospital

I had been admitted to hospital because I could not walk. I was so bad I wasn't able to bathe myself and I needed a wheelchair. My daughter often came to visit me even though she was working and had my granddaughter to look after, but she would make the effort to come, nevertheless. My ex-boyfriend would have made the effort to come and see me, but he lived so far away. But he is a good man.

I remember the doctor telling me I had nearly died, and if it hadn't been for my daughter calling for an ambulance, then it might have been too late. I had been staying at my daughter's house when I had collapsed, and the next thing I remember was lying on a hospital bed. I couldn't even remember being taken into the ambulance. I felt no pain, but I was sweating, and I wanted to move, but the surgeon insisted I stay in bed. To make matters worse, this had occurred during the early hours of the morning, so my daughter had to return home so she could get ready for work.

My daughter had not been allowed to come into the hospital when I had been admitted, but she returned the following day and came into the ICU to see me.

"Mom, what have they done to you?" she said. There was still blood on the sheets, and there were needles lying in the drains.

I could see my daughter's face that she was hurting for me, and I felt for her, too. I felt numb and sick. After the operation I was taken to a side room where I was put into bed and given intramuscular pain killers. The pain could be severe at times, and the doctors and nurses would come to see me regularly although I was only allowed visitors when I was feeling up to it.

I was put in an intensive care unit and therefore I was only allowed minimal visitors, and I wondered if I had been like any of the nurses who were taking care of me. Even people from church came to see me. I could not move for a while, confined to my bed and a wheelchair, it took a long time for my brain to engage with my feet.

My ex-boyfriend did not come to visit me for months, which was sad considering I had initially been fighting for my life. He could be helpful at times, but he was not there, and I missed him dearly. I knew I had to get better and therefore I had to help myself if I was going to get out of here. I tried to walk as often as I could or would be allowed to. I didn't want to be confined to hospital any longer, but I was still unwell and not ready to be discharged.

Afterword
On Reflection of My Past

As a care worker you need to be a good listener, less judgemental and above all, be patient. This case had gone on for years, which had finally taken its toll on me. My mental state was in a turmoil. I had no money, I was drinking tea for most of the time, and I had started to smoke. I stooped so low that I used to go outside and beg for money to buy cigarettes. The case had gone on for so long and the decision from the court was ongoing.

The panel must not use the findings of another body as a substitute for reaching its own decision on the issues before it. The judgment or findings of another decision-maker on the issues before the panel are not relevant to the panel's decision-making. It may also be unfair for the judgments to significantly influence the tribunal's mind on the crucial issues before it for the same reasons.

On reflection, I wonder how many Christmases or birthdays that I missed with my family or loved ones, trying to entertain people who didn't even have the courtesy to say, 'thank you'. The entire court experience was very traumatic, and nothing came of it. I felt intimidated by the police and the court. I had been brave enough to walk alone, to find peace and justice, but I had failed.

It pains me to give up my career as registered mental health nurse. I worked very hard to get my pin number; I endured many sleepless nights, reading and doing my essays for my portfolio, and raising my children. But I held on.

But despite everything I have gone through, there are times when I wonder if I could return to being a nurse in the future. Overall, I believe that I am a much stronger person now, and therefore have returned to doing jobs that I like and I am hopeful that I will continue working with people that see the best in me.

"In future I want to see the world in a grain of sand.
And a Heaven in a wildflower.
Hold infinity in the palm of your hand
And eternity in an hour..." – *Auguries of Innocence* by William Blakes

I wanted to let people know of my experiences working for the NHS—the suspension, the pain I endured and that feeling of being helpless, and an overall lack of support.

I trained to become a mental health nurse at the University of Wolverhampton. I have learned so much and I have never given up. I have learned to take the positive out of the negative and applied that to my life, which is what drove me to write this story.

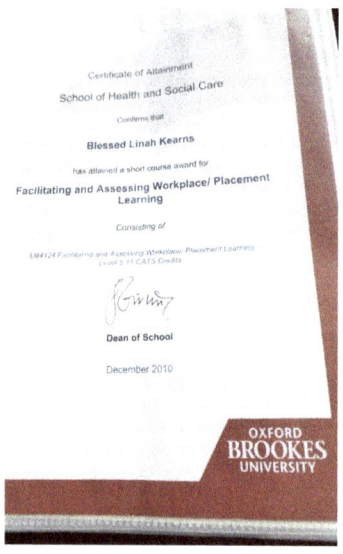

On writing this I would like to thank my daughter for her support and for just being there for me.
Thank you, Gwyneth!
Where is the justice?

Milton Keynes UK
Ingram Content Group UK Ltd.
UKHW021618030823
426158UK00010B/29